By Gary Beck

Novels

Extreme Change
Acts of Defiance
Call to Valor
Sudden Conflicts
Crumbling Ramparts
Flare Up
Raise High the Walls

Still Defiant
State of Rage
Wave Length
Protective Agency
Obsess
Flawed Connections

Poetry

Expectations
Days of Destruction
Dawn in Cities
Assault on Nature
Songs of a Clerk
Civilized Ways
Conditioned Response
Displays
Perceptions
Fault Lines
Tremors
Virtual Living
Perturbations
Blossoms of Decay
Rude Awakenings
Blunt Force

Remission of Orde
Contusions
Transitions
Earth Links
Mortal Coil
Desperate Seeker
Too Harsh For Pastels
Temporal Dreams
Severance
Redemption Value
Fractional Disorder
Disruptions
Ignition Point
Learning Curve
Resonance
Turbulence

Play Collections

The Big Match and other one act plays
Collected Plays of Gary Beck Volume I
Plays of Aristophanes translated then directed by Gary Beck
Collected Plays of Gary Beck Volume II
Four Plays by Moliere Translated then Directed by Gary Beck

Short Story Collections

A Glimpse of Youth
Now I Accuse and other stories
Dogs Don't Send Flowers and other stories

Essays

Collected Essays of Gary Beck

Turbulence

by

Gary Beck

To Arla and Rob whose lives reflect turbulence

Love, Dad

Poems from Turbulence have appeared in:

Active Muse, Bard (Atlantean Publishing, Bewildering Stories, Bindweed Magazine (Heavenly Flower Publishing), BlogNostics, Cabildo Quarterly, Dissident Voice, El Portal, I Am Not A Silent Poet, Indian Periodical, Kingdom in the Wild, Mad Swirl, Modern Literature, Neuro Logical, Nine Muses Poetry, Oddball Magazine, Page & Spine, Peeking Cat Literary Magazine, Plum Tree Tavern, Poetry Leaves, Poetry Life & Times, Pure Slush (Bequem Publishing), Runcible Spoon, Scimitar Magazine (Wolfian Press), Setu Magazine, The Chicago Record, The Magnolia Review, The Nashwaak Review, The Stray Branch, Tuck Magazine, Wax Poetry & Art International, Winamop Magazine, WineDrunk SideWalk, Ygdrasil Journal

Contents

Abusers

I think about the butterfly
a beautiful creature,
nature at its finest
that goes through a birth cycle
as complicated as most
in the unique process
that continues life
for all creatures,
harming no one
fulfilling its role
in the scheme of things,
pollinating,
a brief existence
then abruptly gone.
Yet its short life
is callously ended
by cruel collectors,
murdering the innocent
to pin them on a wall.

Rapt

This morning I smelled hyacinth.
If I stayed near it long enough
it might have driven me mad,
permeating my senses,
driving out thoughts, feelings
out of my seduced control,
swirling with intoxication
far more intimate
then man-made perfume,
leading me to wonder
about our vanities
requiring so many scents.

Downfall

I walk the streets of Dream City,
see the homeless on every corner
cardboard signs proclaiming need,
yet few stop to give alms.
I listen to the people I pass
speaking foreign languages.
I carefully look around
and the city is familiar,
A shock. It's not Calcutta!
It may not look it anymore
but I'm in America,
becoming a third world country.
So many have fallen
so far, so fast,
I barely recognize my land.
The capitalists may as well give away
the Statue of Liberty,
the inspiring French gift,
not much different now
from the Eiffel Tower,
a tourist attraction.

Rights Violators

Early this morning
I heard the birds singing.
What happened to Spring?
What happened to Spring?
One warm day fooled them.
They shed their feathers
now they're shivering
caught by climate change.
They may or may not
survive sudden chill.

Babes in Arms

The avenues of our cities
teem with enraged children
protesting gun violence
violating our schools,
nurturing grounds for the future.
The righteous cries fill the air
demanding safety measures
to protect our schools
from insane disruption.
Yet this noble cause,
a genuine children's crusade,
is tragically doomed to failure
as are all crusades,
because they do not satisfy
the needs of the privileged.

Cold Spell

Winter chill lingers on
stiffening the bones
deceived by almost Spring
into expecting warmth.
The long tormenting cold
smirks at down clad bodies
still not adapted
to freezing days.

Disorder

In the city of decay
the collapsing streets
sag under the anger
of urban traffic
urgent for destinations
timely arrival prevented
by unregulated construction
overwhelming traffic,
foot, car, bus, truck,
all clamoring for passage
hardly willing
to let others pass,
crammed together
in discordant assemblage.

City Sight

The cranes are flying,
not elegant birds,
but heavy machinery
raising buildings to the sky.
They neither tire from elevation,
nor weary from exertion,
having a function of their own
for observant people
who appreciate the city.

Ah, Peace

Another serene day.
The park is filled with tourists,
families, students, workers.
The carousel is turning,
the Yoga class is stretching,
some are playing chess, other games.
Many sit relaxing,
drinking coffee, chatting.
Calm prevails.
Suddenly there's a loud noise.
Everybody freezes,
looks around in alarm,
ready to run.
Another loud noise.
But someone yells:
'It's only a delivery man',
this time not delivering
uninvited death.

Vestiges

The winds of change
now blow so fast
many can't keep up.
Those left behind
become the plebes,
lumpen proletariat,
legions of the unwashed
who in a kinder age
would build a life
for family, kids,
now abandoned
by the tide of greed.

Anonymous Tree

The cherry blossoms have fallen.
They will not bloom again
for another year.
If one does not recognize
the cherry tree when green,
one would never know
the beauty it displayed

Transit is Consistent

In 1654
it took Peter Stuyvesant
almost an hour
to get to work
in what would later be
New York City.

In 1777
it took Isaac Sears
almost an hour
to get to work
you know where.

In 1947
surprise!
It took Fiorello La Guardia
45 minutes
to get to work
in N.Y.C.

Yet in 2018
Why?
It still took
almost an hour
to get to work
in…

Abusers II

Human babies so frail
helpless for months
to manage much
except crawl, mewl,
totally dependent
on caretakers
to feed, protect, cherish.
Yet throughout history
they have been abandoned,
sacrificed, slaughtered,
but not like recent times
mindlessly murdered
by boyfriend, husband,
in senseless acts
that ended the lives
of innocent infants.

Dig Deep

Just because they're down in the mines,
a difficult, demanding job,
it doesn't mean they're dumb.
Smarter miners know beyond doubt
coal mines won't open again
and the jobs won't be coming back.
It's easier to cut off a mountain top
to get at valuable coal
even if it destroys the earth,
rather then dig deep, expensive holes
and employ lots of miners
for high wages and benefits
that does not profit the owners
who do not care what harm they do
as long as they make more money.
Hopefully the smarter miners
will help elect a new President
who won't lie that he's bringing back jobs.

Give Us Your...

The melting pot is broken.
The last tendrils of unity
submerge in alien neighborhoods
subtracted by foreign languages
further separating peoples
fraying the promise of joining together
for immigrants from all walks
building one nation,
with a promise like no other,
as we watch the ebbing away
of the American Dream.

Vistas

I no longer know
how to relate to history.
When I was young
they taught simplistic stuff
which fooled most of the students
most of the time,
until the Cold War
changed the mindsets
of innocent kids
cowering under desks.
Simple beliefs no longer had answers
for questioning intelligence.
The pace of life accelerated.
Even though we lived longer
existence became more complex
as capitalists separated
the rich from the poor,
computer technology separated
those who could compute
from those who couldn't adapt.
And the people were divided
by wealth, caste, ethnicity
and the lords of profit knew gladness,
for the illusion of democracy
that grated on the privileged
was finally fraying away.

Erasure

Escape from reality
is an American trait.
More then any other people
we have avenues of diversion
that take us away
from ideal functioning,.
too easily obliterated
by tv programming, the internet,
until we no longer remember
how to do things.

Cold Spell II

Winter lingers on
stubbornly refusing
to allow Spring thaw.
The sparrows sit
on icy benches
crying to a chilled chorus
for warmer days.

Indictment

The administration
with the approval of the President
is separating children from parents
at the Mexican border,
another assault on human decency
one of many sneak attacks
intended to distract the public
from high crimes and misdemeanors
doing irreparable harm
to the fabric of America,
fraying in so many places
from more and more assaults
that erode the future
of our struggling nation,
as our President presents
overwhelming evidence
that he is an enemy of the people.

Waiting Room

The chairs are filled
with the ailing elderly
mortality etched on faces
of diminishing hope,
as their dwindling future beckons
more pain, more discomfort,
expectations reduced to twinges
of remembrance of vigorous days,
now existence measured
by time in front of the tv.

The Building of America

Most of us don't know
or have forgotten
there once wasn't an America.
The 'native Americans'
may have gotten here first
but they weren't native to the land,
immigrants from a distant land mass.
no longer hospitable.

Brief visitations
by Vikings, explorers
did not impact the land
until the Spanish reached the West Coast
and the Dutch reached the East Coast.
They both began to depredate the land,
cheat, enslave, kill, transmit diseases
to the local communities
who could not cope
with advanced civilization.

More and more arrived
in the New World
didn't disrupt the ecology too much.
After all, how much damage
could some greedy Europeans do
to a vast wilderness?
But they certainly started to reduce
the Indian population.

America today
cannot conceive
of the endless resources
that tempted the English, French
on the East Coast.
Huge forests,
not like the Old World
mostly tamed,
teeming animal life
for food and profit.

Maybe the Dutch
weren't overly ambitious.
Maybe the Spanish
weren't as vigorous.
The English erupted
subduing the wild
planting, planting, planting,
building villages, towns, cities,
even the underclass
filling their bellies
as they couldn't in Merry Old…

Then the Europeans made a crucial mistake.
Unlike the other colonies
of criminals, refuse, the dispossessed,
substantial people,
Englishman of worth and stature
relocated to the colonies,
prospered
and still considered themselves
English citizens.

So when the servants of the crown
inflicted onerous demands
leveled unreasonable taxes,
the descendants
of Roundheads and Cavaliers
insisted on their rights
and when they were ignored by the crown
began to resist
and it became revolution.

Now the servants of the crown
completely forgot
that the ancestors of the colonists
were warlike and determined
and their offspring
learned the art of war
first fighting the Indians,
then fighting the French
for possession of the land
that no longer felt like it belonged
to a crotchety king far away.

When England lost
what they didn't recognize
as a civil war
but treated as a rebellion,
their world turned upside down
and a new nation was born
with endless room for growth,
uncharted vistas for expansion
with no obligation
to any other nation.

Then began the greatest land grab
in the history of civilization.
After securing what had been
the territory of the crown,
a huge tract of undeveloped land
big enough to lose England
many times over.
The best grab of all,
after the 13 colonies of course,
was the Louisiana Purchase in 1803
scammed from Napoleon,
First Consul of France for life,
paid for with borrowed money
that took a long time to pay back.

So all at once a simple treaty
doubled the size of America
and the lust for acquisition
burned bright in the hearts of the grabbers
who had to make all kinds of deals
with still to be feared Spain
who owned different parts of America,
but were bribed out of Louisiana
by our promise not to grab Texas.
In 1819 we got Florida
and established the boundary of the U.S
through the Rocky Mountains
and west to the Pacific Ocean.

The last huge land grab
on our democratic continent
that now spread from sea to shining sea,
unlike today, when pollution

and endless amounts of plastic
have worn away the shine
was in a carefully provoked war
with Mexico just a few years after
the new nation got rid of Spain. Why?
Because we annexed Texas
in 1845, that didn't belong to us.

At the cost of a minimum of blood
we got what then became
New Mexico, Nevada, Arizona,
Texas, California, Washington,
Oregon and parts of what would later be
Oklahoma, Colorado,
Kansas, Wyoming, Montana… Whew!
A lot to digest.

We had a great appetite
for acquisition
and a huge continent
to snatch more territory
by hook, crook, force.
The British conceded Oregon
in 1846, to conquer in India,
other places requiring resources
consuming too much
to struggle with the young upstart.

We got Minnesota
in 1849,
another Brit concession.
Then we bought, after veiled threats,
another piece of Mexico

in 1853,
the Gadsden Purchase
a sizable chunk
that became part of
Arizona, New Mexico,
the last substantial
territorial acquisition
in the contiguous United States.

Then the great public issue,
slavery,
inflamed many of the people
in the ongoing struggle
over which new territory
would be free,
which would be slave.
And the Northern mercantile barons
and the Southern agricultural barons
contested who would rule our nation,
dominance more important
then compromise.

So a great clash began
far more destructive
then loyalists versus rebels.
And battle ruled the land
on a massive scale
only seen before,
in the Napoleonic Wars.
And each side was determined
to prevail against the enemy,
fellow Americans.

After enough blood was shed
to fertilize the land
many times over
and the South was reduced
by force of arms,
economic constraints,
until the will to resist
was overwhelmed
by superior resources,
a terrible war came to an end
and a divided land
had to make its way past conflict.

The ground was barely dry
from the bloody battles
of the Civil War
when we made what might have been
the first honest acquisition
of a vast chunk of territory,
Alaska, purchased from Russia,
in 1867, for 7 million,
sold because she was afraid
Great Britain would snatch it
still eager for spoils
after the Crimean War.
So they called it 'Seward's Folly'
too ignorant to realize
the resources in the huge territory.

Alaska was mostly ignored
until the great gold strike
that sent thousands north
lusting for fortunes, adventure,

whatever call they answered
to a wild turbulent land
where few prospered
many died, most were disappointed
but towns grew, despite harsh clime,
and people began to flourish
until they led normal lives,
with schools, jobs, roads, taxes
and became part of America.

It took a while
before the enmity of war
dissipated
and much suffering
marked the healing process,
as bitter foes
slowly reunited,
putting the horrors behind them
and thousands of warriors
carried their guns West
to take land from the Indians.

Tribe after tribe crumbled
was devastated
by battle, disease,
insufficient resources
to resist incursion
by greedy, land hungry men
unleashed without restriction
on Native Americans
unaccustomed to modern warfare
who quickly succumbed
to determined settlers,

helped by U.S. troops,
eager to plant roots
in a new way of life.

Consolidation
began to fill in the land.
Also industrial barons
grew rich and powerful
and exercised more control
of the body politic.
The nation grew more crowded
and the lords of profit were hungry
for greater gains,
but we had run out of room
and the lust for expansion
turned our appetites
on declining Spain.

So with a rallying cry:
'Remember the Maine',
an American warship
blown up in Cuban waters
in mysterious circumstances,
the owners of America
declared war on Spain
and after a short fight
with an enfeebled foe,
more men lost to disease
than in battle,
we emerged victorious
from our first foreign war
of aggression, acquisition.

And the loot was glorious.
Cuba, Puerto Rico, the Philippines,
little islands here and there
including one grand prize,
Hawaii, annexed
against the wishes of course
of native Hawaiians
unconcerned with our desire
to become a Pacific power
and continue growth,
one way or another
of the American empire.

The old dogs of Europe
still didn't recognize
our greedy aspirations
for a bigger share
of the wealth of the world
and didn't pay much attention.
But we were beginning to swagger
and T.R. built a 'White Fleet',
sent it sailing around the world
announcing to those who noticed
we were ready to play
on a bigger stage.

We annexed Guam,
a convenient coaling station
for our ships in the Pacific
advancing our interests,
although uninvited.
So when Japan went to war
with the Russian bear

and an oriental upstart
defeated a western power
T.R. became a mediator
and alienated the Japanese
by denying sufficient fruits
of a glorious victory.

The 'Great Power' struggles
for colonies in Asia, Africa,
pitted the English and French
early exploiters
of native peoples,
against young Germany
lusting for expansion
in foreign lands,
frequently denied
by those who got there first.
Interests collided.
Tensions mounted.
Unwise heads couldn't control
the rush to conflict.

Dogs of War began to bay.
Huge armies mobilized
and a great clash spread
across much of the world.
The owners of America
observed carefully,
saw they couldn't gain colonies
and realized they could buy
a different kind of empire
where the flag didn't fly,
but the dollar ruled.

So once the players were exhausted
and owed us millions for war goods
we intervened and exported war.

And when the great war ended
we had infiltrated many lands.
We may not have played a major role
in negotiating the peace
but we firmly established
the role of the dollar.
The owners of America
had a lot to digest
and ordered the people
to stop drinking hard liquor,
distracting us from the goals
of the lords of profit
to dominate the world.

The enemies we defeated
in brutal battles, hated us.
The friends we saved
from bitter defeat, hated us.
But we mostly ignored
international ill will
as we plotted to become
a world power.
So when the usual combatants
went to war again
we stayed on the sidelines,
lending lots of money
until the planes came
out of the rising sun
and bombed us into World War II.

After devastating defeats
we built a great war machine
that dwarfed anything in the past
and sent ships, planes, tanks, men
to battle in many lands.
And what our troops didn't conquer
the dollar dominated,
compelling acceptance everywhere,
as we bestrode the world
presenting a benevolent mien
that was generally oppressive,
just not as brutal as some masters.

The coffers of the lords of profit
knew fullness from the war effort
that required everything for victory.
So when the guns fell silent
and the troops came home
we stopped building ships, planes, tanks,
and the endless flow of money
suddenly began to diminish.
For without fierce enemies
what need of a massive military?
Fortunately for the owners of America
the dreaded 'Red Menace' reared its head
just in time to rearm for the 'Cold War'.

The owners of America
looked upon their works
that capital had built
and they knew fullness.
Out of benevolent neglect
or just plain indifference

they allowed millions of returning soldiers
to go to college, become middle class,
enjoy prosperity as never before
as their children had comforts.
Yet the parents submerged in possessions
and didn't teach their children values,
so the offspring of abundance
ignored superficial teachings
and wallowed in indulgence.

The powerful nation
that conquered the world
established an empire
military and economic,
as the dollar ruled everywhere.
But the factories and oil companies
that exported to the world
grew obsolete, less profitable,
so the owners abandoned the people
who had toiled to make them rich,
moved their businesses to other lands,
eradicated the blue collar jobs
that allowed men and women
material comforts, pride in their labor,
opportunity for their children.

Then our society knew radical change.
The children of the parents of prosperity
rebelled against college authority,
then protested the Vietnam War
with uncompromising demands
ignored by the lords of profit,
besieged their government,

forced the sitting President
not to seek reelection,
made huge, outraged demonstrations,
but when the war finally ended
submerged into the security
of the welcoming system.

The long, slow slide to decay
began without much notice.
As factory jobs disappeared
unions became smaller, weaker,
now dependent on the bosses
for fewer and fewer jobs.
The traditional trade route
from upper lower class
to lower middle class
and an easier life
narrowed from a superhighway
to a one lane blacktop
of diminishing traffic.

As the people became poorer
the nation had increasing debt.
Limited wars against weak foes
brought huge profits to our masters
that they didn't share with most of us.
More and more stores and restaurants closed
depriving the technologically unfit
of accessible jobs, livelihoods
while robots and computers
determined the workplace of the future,
if our brief, transient empire
survives the present.

Lost Soul

A homeless woman
sat on the sidewalk
in New York City,
Fifth Avenue
and 42nd Street,
ravaged by time,
poverty, mental illness,
we do not know the cause
of her eroded state,
since we only see
her desiccated body
and a cardboard sign:
'Need someone to care'.

Hazardous Dreams

A growing phenomenon
is how many people
walk the streets
who may not have turned on
but certainly tuned in,
wearing headsets
listening to whatever
oblivious to the usual sounds
of a complex city
where the only early warning
of impending danger
might be a missed sound
that does not penetrate
distracting rap, pop.

Midtown Sprawl

Like any third world country
the homeless have been abandoned
in wealthy New York City.
The poverty population
used to be mostly hidden
in the outer boroughs,
or Manhattan slums.
Now that it is normal
for legions of the dispossessed
to proliferate anywhere,
the homeless sit on city streets
with cardboard signs announcing need
inevitably ignored
in a time of endless demand,
given further excuse
by half naked bodies
supine on the sidewalk.

Nice Change

This weekend I saw cherry blossoms
forsythia, hyacinth, daffodils,
all giving the illusion of Spring,
even though it was cold.
Then I saw Robins,
the first time since last year
and knew the sullen days
of winter were departing.

'Tis of Thee

Enemies threaten us from abroad.
Violence rages through the land.
The Senate cannot govern
and shuts down the government
because they can't agree.
The wealthy get richer,
the poor get poorer.
Our leaders allow more waste
to be dumped in our rivers.
And the endless wars
consuming our children, our treasure.
The list of woes goes on and on.
But then I put down my book,
the Decline and Fall of the Roman Empire,
and I can only wonder
if history is repeating itself
as barbarian hordes proliferate
within our very walls.

No Warning

Strong winds blow harder and harder.
City dwellers huddle in doorways
sheltered from flying debris.
Snow begins to fall
faster and faster.
Traffic slows,
comes to a standstill.
The snow gets deeper.
Emergency services slow down
unprepared for a blizzard.
People bring out skis and sleds
enjoying winter despite its wrath.
But the snow keeps falling.
Police and ambulances stop responding.
The ailing struggle to the hospitals.
Some don't make it.
It continues to snow.
Even the skiers stop.
It gets colder and colder.
Another day goes by.
Drifts are four feet high.
Fires break out.
The Fire Department can't respond.
The snow keeps fires from spreading.
Suddenly the power fails
leaving the city blacked out.
The elderly begin to die.
Everyone sits in darkness
wondering if they'll see light again.

Pity the Lesser Haves

The wealthy have a wealth gap
as the top one-hundredth of the 1 percent
leave the merely very rich behind
in the purchase of art, diamonds, yachts
while the rising tide is lifting mega-yachts,
orders for 300 footers to a record high,
costing about $250 million,
more then most millennials can afford,
also denied the pleasure of large-cabin jets,
so they can only seethe with envy
at the bigger, better purchases
of their economic superiors.

The Roar of Spring

Winter refuses to pack up,
get out of town
let a warm front move in
cheering chilled people
more then tired of the cold,
eager to put away
down coats, heavy gloves
see trees turn green
lifting the spirits
of the shivering masses.

Let Madness Reign

We can easily understand
why chaos reigns in our troubled land,
for the owners of our country
require instability
to maintain their positions
without suffering restrictions
on their exercising power,
while our beloved children cower
in vulnerable, defenseless schools,
unprotected by the adult fools
who rave about classroom locks,
arming our children with rocks,
making school assaults a trifle
by a mad kid with a rifle.

State of the Union

Not caring for others
has become endemic
in our troubled society
ravaged by poverty,
a growing disease
afflicting millions
at a terrible time
of diminishing opportunity
for the children of need,
deprived of services
that allow a better life,
indifference of the rich
arbitrarily condemning
so many youth
to a dismal future.

Uncertain Times

It is April seventh in New York City.
37 degrees F. Damp. Dank. Snow expected.
I have not seen a Robin,
provoking my fear
that they have abandoned
the good old U.S.A.
betrayed by the E.P.A.
We self-elected our species
custodians of the Earth,
yet between global warming,
climate change, loss of habitat,
wanton consumption
of natural resources,
and the usual depredations
of war, disease, crime, poverty,
our hope for the future
lies in space travel
to habitable planets,
where we'll ravage the new home
just as we've devastated the old.

The Road to...

Tensions rise across the globe
as state and non -state actors
devise more violent schemes
to threaten their enemies,
undermine those who can resist,
intimidate the weaker,
and terrorize the helpless.
During these troubled times
the American ship of state
guided by an ignoramus
who knows little, respects nothing,
burdens us with growing debt,
erodes the middle class,
fraying our institutions,
until the hope of the future
is dangerously imperiled.

Cold Spell III

The sparrows sang a dirge this morning.
Spring has died. Spring has died.
I sympathize with them.
It's the first week of April
and it's 35 F. outside.
My old bones feel like mourning
but like the sparrows
I can't control the weather,
so I bundle up,
go about my business,
resigned to waiting
for warmer days.

Going Downhill

Our country is fortunate
with an ego-filled ignoramus,
a Mussolini type
rather than a Hitler,
who may aggravate many
with bombast and petty spite
but we'll probably survive
the worst he can do
another sad indicator
of the degeneracy
of the Presidency

So Proudly We Once Hailed

It has been a long time
since I expected
    democracy.
    After all
the rich buy anything they want
including politicians,
leaving my poor country
    oppressed
by the corrupt and evil
not allowing
    even the illusion
    of freedom.

Dollars at Work

The bombs and missiles fall
on Syria, Iraq,
Afghanistan, other lands,
sent by America
whether to quell enemies
or consume war materials
that must be replaced
profitably
to perpetuate
capitalism
and those who gain by it,
regardless of the suffering
inflicted on everyone else.

Brief Beauty

The wisteria is fading,
a fragile life,
not as long as mine.

Abusers III

Hunters roam the earth
perversely seeking trophies
of all kinds of animals,
most not dangerous to man.
The few that are fierce
are hopelessly outgunned
by ruthless predators
willing to exterminate
the last of a species
so they can mount a head
on an indifferent wall
mindlessly displaying
the slaughtered victim
so all can admire
the mighty hunter.

Perspective

Another school shooting.
A calculating teen
violently invades
what should have been
a safe learning center.
Except for the aggrieved,
it's quickly forgotten.
A disturbed man
kills his girlfriend's baby
because it cried too loud.
Yet it's quickly forgotten.
Women charge a prominent man
with sexual abuse
and the outrage is deafening.
The case goes on and on
titillating the people,
far more important
then the slaughter of children.

Progress

Once the telephone
was a wonder instrument
that no one took for granted,
few understanding
how it worked.
Now the Iphone
is an incredible device
that everyone takes for granted,
fewer understanding
how it works.

As We Sink

The trees are green.
Flowers are blooming.
The birds are singing
cheerfully.
It's hard to imagine
disasters everywhere,
natural, man made.
We can't control
an erupting volcano,
all we can do
is flee the lava.
What's more frightening
in a different way
is a bad President
out of control,
wrecking the future
of a declining empire,
callously betrayed
by greedy capitalists
with no concern
for the fate of the people.

Onus

Throughout the world
people suffer
from endless afflictions,
some made by man,
some natural,
all restricting
the pleasures of life.
So when evil men
do terrible deeds
and make things worse
it's another burden
that only adds
to our daily pain.

Shock

A grudge festers
year in, year out,
reaches boiling point,
leads to detonation.
Someone goes postal,
invades an office,
shoots bystanders
with no concern
for innocence, guilt,
just blind anger
delivering death
unexpectedly.

Streaming

Disconnectedness
affects so many,
saturated
with information
from the internet,
the fountain of knowledge
diffused electronically,
insufficient questioning
building blind acceptance.

Deceptions

Controversial issues
stir those who care,
those looking to agitate.
Treatment of migrants
currently arouses indignation,
especially the plight of children
separated from parents,
leading to angry protests
a credit to caring Americans,
who may not realize
the harsh actions
may be meant to distract
from Presidential crimes.

Rape and Pillage

The system I grew up with,
a democratic ideal
of checks and balances
to preserve basic rights,
has been loudly overturned
by an ignorant, dangerous leader
who knows not the harm he does.
He collaborates with destruction
of the environment,
undermines the economy
with irresponsible trade wars,
betrays the American people
by diminishing opportunities,
and shatters the international order
that has prevented World War III
since 1946.
Is he evil? Insane? Both?
What else could explain
his assault on the nation?

Traffic Jam

Sirens frequently go off
in large cities,
police, fire, ambulances.
Once we moved out of the way
so emergency services got through.
Now many are reluctant to move
unwilling to give up their place,
urgent to reach destinations.
Of course they don't realize
that if they were in the ambulance
in a race for life and death
the traffic obstructions
would insure they wouldn't arrive alive.

Motives

It's almost reassuring
in a society gone mad
when someone has a reason
for a deadly rampage.
We grow accustomed
to mindless assaults
on schools, churches,
other gathering places
where we presume safety,
until fatally reminded
by sudden attack.

Closed Doors

A protester scales
Lady Liberty,
who no longer welcomes
alien intruders,
the portals slammed shut
to undernourished newcomers
urgent to enter
the promised land,
definitely better
then where they came from,
finding it difficult to understand
why they're not wanted.

The Road to Disaster

The President reflects
the nature of the people,
at least enough to elect him.
As we reel under his assaults
on the economy
creating a bigger and bigger
poverty class,
insane attacks
on the environment
poisoning our waters,
alienating friends, allies,
until they no longer trust us
and may not support us
in our time of need,
as we are victims of greed,
stupidity, insanity,
betraying our tomorrows.

Good Trip

Tourists come to New York City,
some apprehensive
after watching violent films, tv.
Many are pleasantly surprised
by New Yorker's courtesy,
willing to give directions,
polite, some saying hello,
not like some rough streets
in distant homelands,
every outing hazardous,
vacations in the U.S.A
a true relief.

Mindwash

The myth that government
is the servant of the people
promoted by the media
and the radical right
who brainwash the susceptible
and thoroughly delude many
who do not understand
the real enemy of the people
are the lords of profit,
who manipulate everyone
and blame others
for whatever goes wrong,
so they can do whatever they want
regardless of the harm
to today and tomorrow.

Identity Shift

The television age
spawned conformity
as many viewers
depending on income
bought the same clothes,
dressed the same way,
ate the same food
until it's difficult to tell
tourists from natives
in Western countries.

Harsh Times

Some of us
look for explanations
why so many things,
the economy,
the environment,
foreign affairs,
are going so wrong,
fixed on endless conceptions
that the owners of America
cared about the nation,
cared about the people.
It is too painful
for most of us to accept
that the determiners of the future
only care about themselves.

Ideal

Each day I curse tv
for the filth it pumps
into my view.
But I must watch news,
however brutal,
as I view the world
mankind debases.
Then I see the rescue
of endangered children
from a ravenous cave
eager to devour them,
and I am reminded
of the nobility of man.

More Guns

The National Rifle Association,
the most fanatic defenders
of the right to bear arms,
went to court to bring suit
to stop a state legislature
from raising the age to buy guns
from eighteen to twenty one,
citing the Second Amendment.

In deference to gun manufacturers
who aren't evil death merchants
and only want to make money,
we should lower the age requirement
to buy guns to thirteen,
for after all the amendment
doesn't say anything about age,
and why shouldn't thirteen year olds
belong to a well regulated militia.

If only old Tom Jefferson
could see the militias today,
wearing camis, carrying AR-15s,
ready for armed response
against their enemy, the government,
too ignorant to recognize
the real enemy are the rich.

But if they understood about the rich
they'd be commies, or socialists,

rather then heroic patriots.
So let's sell guns to kids
You never know. Some of them
might be responsible gun users.

Holiday Cheer

Families with children
don't notice the cold
on the special day
of the wearing of the green.
Few know why its green
but it doesn't spoil the pleasure
kilted bagpipers give
squalling away,
delighting the crowds
with their colorful march.

Changeable

The sparrows have begun to sing
that finally it's Spring. It's Spring!
But it seems they sang too soon
and now they'll sing a different tune,
for suddenly it started snowing,
winter winds continue blowing.

Rash Attack

Our planes attacked Syria today.
Our ships fired missiles.
The President gloated
and boasted about the military
with his usual bombast,
oblivious to the consequences
of arbitrary attacks
on vulnerable enemies
including terrorist retaliation
to punish evil America
for interfering with another country,
a violation of their sovereignty
blatantly ignored
by an ignorant leader
with no idea
what he may have unleashed.

Harbinger

The sun is high in the sky.
The temperature is rising.
Green buds sprouted on the trees.
The birds are singing happily.
We have already forgotten
the snowstorm the first day of Spring.
Now we are ready to enjoy
shirt sleeves in warm weather.

Homeless Quatrain

In the park the homeless wait
hoping for a change of fate
that never comes when they're alive
abandoned by a callous state.

Can It Be?

Dogwood is blooming everywhere.
Daffodils are blooming everywhere.
A scrawny cherry tree
is working like wild
to put out its aroma.
So much of Nature
seems to be doing its stuff
for a beautiful Spring,
yet its just a few degrees
above freezing.

Velocity

City streets are overcrowded.
Traffic creeps from street to street.
Delays to destinations
consume so much working time
it wastes vital resources.
The practical solution
efficient mass transit
doesn't seem to matter
to short sighted officials
unable to conceive
of a long term plan
to get us quickly
from place to place.

Changeable II

The first warm day of Spring.
The sun is shining.
The birds are singing.
Trees are beginning to leaf.
People are wearing short sleeves.
Everyone is taking advantage
of a balmy day
unwilling to believe
it will be cold tomorrow.

Third World

People wander through the park
aimless, relaxed, cheerful,
enjoying the moment
without the faintest idea
our frayed society
is careening to disaster.
Unlike other times
in history
when coincidence,
miracle, proper actions
saved the day,
the paucity of our leaders
painfully reminds us
they cannot help us
and most don't ever care.

Behavior Pattern

Human nature
is often contrary,
people refusing to listen,
when given instructions
even when it's life or death,
congregating socially
in the narrowest part of the sidewalk
so it's difficult to pass,
like the self-entitled
who think they're privileged
expecting preferential treatment
trapped in middle class illusion,
and do not know nor care
that most of the world
is trapped in poverty
without opportunity.

Intrusion

Springtime in the park.
Only the homeless are overdressed
wearing all their clothing,
carrying all their possessions
because they have nowhere to go
except a temporary bench,
made uncomfortable
by the suspicious stares
of the more fortunate.

Abdication

The weakness of a country
is not determined by the leaders
but from the decay of values,
corruption sponsored by greed,
as our society rots away
and we blame others
because too many of us
have forgotten our responsibilities
to the nation.

Deviance

Human behavior
is the strangest
of all creatures,
far more complicated
with a vast range
of emotions
causing endless conflict,
never allowing peace,
greed, ambition, lust,
all driving events
that lead to destruction
for millions,
year after year,
the cleverest inventions
bringing death
instability,
insecurity normal
since man climbed down
from the trees.

I. Q. Test

An actor on tv
cursed the President.
Many viewers thought it was funny.
The President meets Kim
and announces he trusts him.
It's clear which one is crazier
and which one is dumber,
but there's no question
of who's more dangerous.

Turmoil

Disasters sweep the world
causing death and debilitation.
Powerful storms
linger in memory
until prosperity
breeds forgetting.
War ravages many lands
devastating entire peoples
recovery almost impossible
without massive aid
rarely available
to most countries,
unless they have valuable assets
that make them worth saving.

Misconceptions

I heard a phrase today
I never heard before.
'Cultural appropriation'.
It referred to a theatre production
in a foreign country
where the show was canceled
because white actors
played black cotton pickers,
offending profoundly
the African-American ethos
that whites should not play blacks.
Poor white sharecroppers once picked cotton,
so its not beyond ethnic possibility.
Some people are forgetting, or do not know,
an actors job is to fool the audience
into believing he/she is the character.
An actor should play roles
according to his/her skills and talent.
We wouldn't want a good black actor
 to be deprived of playing Hamlet, Ophelia,
just because they're black.

Winding Down

In the nursing home
seniors come and go,
not lingering long
before the last move
to final resting place.

Dissatisfied

The hot days of summer
arrived without warning
and those who complained all winter
about the unpleasant cold
are griping again
about the unpleasant heat.
These people are exponents
of the complaining class.
Fortunately they have no power
or they'd bring a class action suit
against Mother Nature.

Despoilers

Intersection of ideas
rarely leads to severe conflict,
while intrusion of values
provokes confrontation.
Most humans prefer peace and quiet.
Some are greedy, ambitious,
inflict their will on others
poisoning the society
that allows the good life.

Thwarted Hordes

Cities were formed
for protection
against marauders,
prototype walls
built to prevent
nomadic horsemen
form riding down
defenseless farmers.
It took a while
for nomads to realize
they couldn't go where they wanted
and though still feared
were sometimes manageable.

Park Riff

In the park
the tourists come and go
spending the Euro,
eyes filled with delight
at the frequent sight
of purchasable goods.

Blemish

What has my country come to
once revered for freedom,
the promise of democracy,
when our President
who does not represent the majority
meets the Russian President,
alone, without anyone to monitor
what he might give away
of the American heritage.
Suspicion of his motives
is triggered by rumors of blackmail
by the ruthless Russians,
who purportedly have video
of Trump cavorting
with Russian hookers,
shaming our nation.

Petulant Prez

President Trump
threatens angrily
to shut down the government
unless he's given money
to build a wall
preventing Mexicans
from crossing the Rio Grande,
sneaking into America
in hope of a better life.
Trump will punish the people
if he doesn't get what he wants,
almost unrestricted
in his abuse of power.